Author:
Jim Pipe studied ancient and modern history at Oxford University, then spent 10 years in publishing before becoming a full-time writer. He has written numerous nonfiction books for children, many on historical subjects. He lives in Dublin with his lovely wife, Melissa.

Artist:
David Antram was born in Brighton, England, in 1958. He studied at Eastbourne College of Art and then worked in advertising for fifteen years before becoming a full-time artist. He has illustrated many children's nonfiction books.

Series Creator:
David Salariya was born in Dundee, Scotland. He has illustrated a wide range of books and has created and designed many new series for publishers both in the UK and overseas. In 1989, he established The Salariya Book Company. He lives in Brighton with his wife, illustrator Shirley Willis, and their son Jonathan.

Editor:
Sophie Izod

Editorial Assistant:
Mark Williams

© The Salariya Book Company Ltd MMVI

Published in Great Britain in 2006 by
The Salariya Book Company Ltd
25 Marlborough Place, Brighton BN1 1UB

ISBN-10: 0-531-18726-8 (Lib. Bdg.)   0-531-18923-6 (Pbk.)
ISBN-13: 978-0-531-18726-5 (Lib. Bdg.) 978-0-531-18923-8 (Pbk.)

Published in 2007 in the United States
by Franklin Watts
An imprint of Scholastic Library Publishing
90 Sherman Turnpike, Danbury, CT 06816

A CIP catalog record for this book is available
from the Library of Congress.

Printed and bound in China.
Printed on paper from sustainable sources.

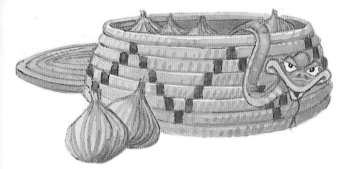

You Wouldn't Want to Be Cleopatra!

Written by
Jim Pipe

Illustrated by
David Antram

Created and designed by
David Salariya

An Egyptian Ruler You'd Rather Not Be

Franklin Watts®
A Division of Scholastic Inc.
NEW YORK • TORONTO • LONDON • AUCKLAND • SYDNEY
MEXICO CITY • NEW DELHI • HONG KONG
DANBURY, CONNECTICUT

Contents

Introduction

You are Cleopatra, a princess living in Egypt 2,000 years ago. Your father is the pharaoh, and you live in Alexandria, the greatest city in the ancient world. Your family has ruled Egypt for almost 300 years, since the conquest of Egypt by your ancestor, Ptolemy. Egypt is a rich country with a glorious past—the pyramids are already 2,500 years old! These are dangerous times, though, and Egypt is in serious trouble, weakened by invasions and bad government. Across the Mediterranean Sea, Roman power is strengthening and Egypt is a rich prize . . .

The famous Pharos lighthouse stood at the entrance to the harbor at Alexandria, one of the Seven Wonders of the Ancient World.

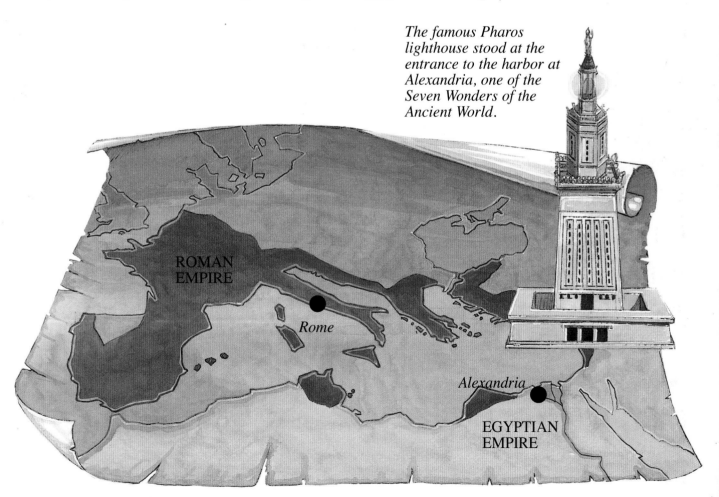

ROMAN
EMPIRE

Rome

Alexandria

EGYPTIAN
EMPIRE

Life on the Run

You are born in 69 BC, and grow up in your father's royal court at Alexandria. Your family is very rich and you live in great comfort, but being the pharaoh's daughter brings its own problems. Your family is not Egyptian but Greek, so it is not popular with ordinary Egyptians at the best of times.

To make matters worse, your father, Ptolemy XII, is a weak and cruel ruler. The people of Alexandria rebel against him and place your elder sister Berenice on the throne. So, at the age of eleven, you are forced to leave home and go on the run with your father. For the next three years, you live in exile abroad, moving around from Rome to Athens to the Greek island of Rhodes as your father looks for help.

BIG WAVE!!

Life as a Princess

PRINCESSES MUST study hard. Egypt already has 3,000 years of history, so there are lots of pharaoh's names to learn! Alexandria also has the biggest library in the ancient world, so there are endless scrolls to read.

SAILING across the Mediterranean is no picnic, especially if you get seasick. Storms and shipwrecks are common and pirates are a menace!

Uh-oh...

Rocks off the starboard bow, captain!

Are we there yet, Dad?

Handy Hint

There may be assassins out to poison you, so get a servant to taste your food first!

BEING RICH means you get to wear beautiful clothes and eat delicious food. Since your father Ptolemy has run off with the family treasure, money is never a problem!

LIFE IS TOUGH IN THE ANCIENT WORLD, even for royalty. Many people do not live past 30. Your own mother died just a year after you were born.

Wail!

Weep!

7

A Family Affair

When you are 14, your father Ptolemy wins his throne back with the help of the Romans. The first thing he does is to behead your sister Berenice for ruling in his place. Welcome home!

Three years later, in 51 BC, your father dies. As the eldest child, you become queen. Great! The bad news is that as a woman you are not allowed to rule on your own, so you have to marry your 12-year-old brother, also called Ptolemy. If this seems strange, you must remember that the god Osiris married his sister Isis, so Egyptians think its OK for royal brothers and sisters to marry each other too. It is also a way of making sure no one outside your family gets a chance to rule.

WHEN IT COMES TO NAMES, your family has no imagination. All the boys are called Ptolemy and all the girls are called Arsinoe, Cleopatra, or Berenice. Your mother was also Cleopatra, as is one of your sisters. Your two brothers are both Ptolemy, like your father Ptolemy XII (and eleven kings before him!).

Na Nah Nah Na Na! I'm pharaoh!

Ptolemy!

Who, me?

Let's see how long this lasts!

Just you wait . . .

Handy Hint

Nicknames are a good way to remember your relatives. Your father Ptolemy has the nickname Auletes, meaning the "flute-player."

Your Delightful Relatives

YOUR ANCESTOR Ptolemy V, nicknamed "Pot Belly," murdered his son, chopped up his body, and served it to the boy's mother, Ptolemy's own sister!

WHEN YOUR SISTER Berenice took the throne, she married a cousin, but then had him strangled so that she could marry another man, Archelaus.

WHEN YOU BECOME queen, you poison one of your younger brothers to allow your son to become king. Tsk, tsk!

It's Tough at the Top

What Are Your Royal Duties?

Temple

RELIGION. Your most important job is keeping the gods happy, especially the hawk-headed sun god, Ra. Build big temples for the gods and make sure your priests offer regular sacrifices to them.

At 18, you are Cleopatra VII, queen of Egypt. For three years you rule without your annoying little brother interfering too much. You're very popular with ordinary Egyptians and like all pharaohs, you are worshipped like a god. People call you "Cleopatra, daughter of Ra."

Being queen, however, is not just about nice clothes, good food, and fast ships. Egypt is a big country and you are responsible for running it. You have thousands of officials working for you and they follow your every command. Meanwhile, you have plans to make Egypt a great empire again. It is going to be a tough job and you realize that you need help from the Romans.

TAXES make you one of the richest people in the world. But you have to manage a big team of officials, some of whom are happy to pocket the money for themselves!

ARMY. The pharaoh is the head of the army, though as a woman you are not expected to fight. But keep an eye on your generals because you need their support.

Down with Cleo!

DROUGHT. Being a goddess is pretty great, but you do get blamed for natural disasters. For two years during your reign, the Nile floods fail. There is a famine and many Egyptians blame you.

A Man's World

As your brother Ptolemy grows older, he becomes more and more bossy. His advisors, led by the wily Pothinus, start plotting against you. They think only men know how to rule. They are also against your plans to become allied with the Romans.

In 48 BC, Pothinus hatches a plot to kidnap you. Luckily, you find out in time and flee the country with your sister Arsinoe. You sail to Syria and then return overland to the Egyptian border, where you gather an army and prepare to attack your brother. Watch out, Ptolemy, the sisters are doing it for themselves!

Isis

Life as a Woman in Ancient Egypt

A TOUGH ACT TO FOLLOW! The Egyptian idea of the perfect woman is the goddess Isis, a devoted wife and mother who sailed the seas to recover her husband's body and brought him back to life after he died.

FREEDOM. In many parts of the ancient world, women have no freedom and are forced to stay at home all day. But Egyptian women can own property, have jobs, or go to the market themselves.

Boys. Who can trust them!

Psst. Never trust a woman!

Handy Hint
Watch your courtiers closely. They can have a lot of power—two courtiers helped your ancestor Ptolemy V take over the throne.

HARD WORK. Noble women can have important jobs such as high priestess or running the royal dining hall. Most women, however, only get to do back-breaking jobs such as working in the fields or weaving cloth.

MOTHERS. The ancient Egyptians like to have large families. When you are looking after seven or eight children, it's hard to find time to do much else.

IN PAINTINGS, rich Egyptian women are shown with pale skin to show that they never have to go out into the sun to work. Rich men are shown with fat bellies to show how much food and drink they can afford!

Use Your Head . . . Win His Heart

n the far side of the Mediterranean, two Roman generals, Julius Caesar and Pompey, are battling it out for control of the Roman Empire. Pompey goes to your brother for help—bad move! Ptolemy thinks that Caesar will win and has Pompey stabbed to death. When Caesar arrives in Alexandria, he is offered Pompey's head as a gift—another bad move! Caesar is disgusted by the betrayal of his former friend. He promptly marches into the city and seizes control of the palace.

What Are Your Talents?

ΚΛΕΟΠΑΤΡΑ

LANGUAGES. You can speak nine languages and are the first Greek ruler to speak Egyptian. Here is your name "Cleopatra" written in ancient Greek (above) and in Egyptian hieroglyphics (left).

KNOW-IT-ALL! A good mathematician, you have also written papyri (paper scrolls made from reeds) about weights and measures, coins, medicine, cosmetics, farming—and magic!

POLITICS. You need to keep a lot of people happy: the Romans, your courtiers, the Greek city-dwellers in Alexandria, and Egyptians living in the countryside. That takes a lot of cunning!

A BIT OF FLATTERY works well—a lot goes even further. According to the historian Plutarch, you know 1,000 different ways to flatter!

That nose is fit for a king!

Caesar invites you and your brother Ptolemy to meet with him to make peace. It's too dangerous for you to enter Alexandria openly—your brother's soldiers will kill you. Instead, you bribe a merchant called Apollodorus to deliver a rug as a present to Caesar. When the rug is unrolled, you tumble out! Using your charm, Caesar soon falls madly in love with you, and who can blame him?

I love surprises!

SURPRISE!

Act Like a Goddess

When Ptolemy sees you and Caesar together the next day, he storms out of the palace. Soon after, Caesar has Ptolemy arrested. Hearing this, Pothinus and your sister Arsinoe, who has switched sides, attack the palace. War rages for six months until Ptolemy dies in battle and Pothinus is executed. At last, you rule alone!

A year or so later, you become a mother. You name your son Caesarion or "Little Caesar." Hoping the Romans will help you build a new Egyptian empire, you go to Rome. Caesar showers you with gifts and adds a beautiful golden statue of you in the temple of Venus. Then disaster strikes . . . Caesar is murdered by his enemies in Rome!

In 44 BC, Julius Caesar was stabbed to death in the Roman senate by more than 60 conspirators, including his old friend Marcus Brutus.

Know Your Gods and Goddesses

As a Greek woman ruling Egypt with a Roman boyfriend, there are lots of different gods to worship. It can get very confusing!

EGYPTIAN. Ra is the king of the gods. Osiris and Isis are the gods of the dead. Other important gods include jackal-headed Anubis; Horus the sky god; and Thoth, god of wisdom.

Handy Hint

Make the most of being worshipped as a goddess. People in ancient times find it easy to accept new gods, and the Egyptian goddess Isis is popular in Rome.

Ra   Osiris   Isis   Anubis   Horus   Thoth

GREEK. Zeus is the king of the gods. His wife is Hera and his children include Athena, goddess of wisdom; Artemis the hunter; and Dionysus, the god of wine and dancing.

ROMAN. Jupiter is the king of the gods, and Juno is his wife. His daughter Venus is the goddess of love and his son Mars is the god of war.

Athena   Artemis   Dionysus

Mars   Venus

Zeus   Hera

Juno   Jupiter

Just How Gorgeous Are You?

TO BE HONEST, you're not that good looking. Like all the women in your family, you have rolls of fat around your neck and a hooked nose. What makes you so attractive is your incredible personality.

Beauty Secrets

YOU ARE EXPECTED to look like a goddess, so it helps to have a few tricks up your sleeve.

MAKEUP. Go heavy on the eyeliner—black eye shadow also protects against the hot Egyptian sun. Paint ochre on your lips to make them red.

HAIR. You have your hair waved and arranged into overlapping layers. This "melon hairstyle" looks so good on you that it starts a new fashion in Rome.

DRESS. In public you wear Egyptian costume. At home you wear simple Greek robes made of soft linen or smooth silk. Luckily, expensive jewelry goes with everything!

TATTOOS. Some Egyptian women have delicate patterns tattooed in henna on their arms, legs, and stomach. But tattoos aren't worn by noble women and should be avoided.

Looking Good

Once more, Egypt is in danger. After Caesar's assassins are killed in battle, Octavian and Mark Antony agree to divide the Roman Empire between them. Antony takes charge of the eastern half of the empire. He needs your money to raise an army, so invites you to visit him in 41 BC.

WOW! You're more beautiful than Venus herself!

You need Antony's help too, so you put on a real show. You arrive on a golden barge with silver oars and sails made from purple silk. The barge is crewed by maids dressed as sea nymphs. You dress as the goddess Venus, flutes and lyres play in the background, and a big cloud of perfume wafts toward Antony on the shore. Poor Antony doesn't stand a chance and quickly falls under your spell!

Handy Hint

Things can get a bit sweaty after a long day in the heat. To smell good, try bathing in scented horse's milk and honey.

You're no dog-faced Anubis yourself.

Party Time!

Antony is 14 years older than you and has spent most of his life in the army. However, you both enjoy the good things in life—big feasts, wild parties, luxury cruises down the Nile, and hunting trips. Both of you have big plans for the future. Antony plans to conquer Parthia, a kingdom in the East. You are still set on becoming Empress of the world.

How to Throw a Good Party

TO SHOW OFF your wealth, you take off one of your priceless pearl earrings. You crush it up and drop it into a goblet of wine vinegar, which dissolves the pearl. Antony gasps in amazement as you gulp down your millions!

FOOD. Guests feast on plates encrusted with jewels. Your cooks roast eight whole boars, one after the other, so that one is ready when you decide it is time to eat.

DRINK. Red wine is popular, though Egyptians also enjoy their beer, which is so thick you need a straw to drink it!

In 40 BC, Antony has to return to Rome, because of an argument with Octavian. He is away for four years. While he is gone, you give birth to twins—a boy and a girl. When Antony returns, you get married.

Handy Hint
Feeling bored? Why not dress up as a servant and run through the town late at night, playing tricks on people.

PERFUME. Create a fragrant atmosphere in the dining room with frankincense, myrrh, and spices.

ENTERTAINMENT. Every good party needs dancers and musicians. At one of your feasts, a Roman official dresses up as a sea god to entertain the other guests.

21

I'm a Celebrity!

n 36 BC, you begin to build a mighty fleet of ships to defend Egypt, while Antony attacks Parthia. Unfortunately, the war is a complete disaster and you rush to Syria to support your husband. On your return home, you narrowly escape death when King Herod tries to kill you as you travel through Judea.

The next year, Antony has more success and conquers the kingdom of Armenia. To celebrate his victory, you organize a spectacular parade. You and Antony sit on golden thrones, dressed as the god Dionysus and the goddess Isis. Your children sit on smaller thrones next to you, and each of them is given a country by Antony. When he hears about this, Octavian is furious, because some of the lands given to your children belong to Rome.

How to Become Famous

MONEY. Send agents all over the Mediterranean to bribe kings and officials at foreign courts.

FESTIVALS. Every four years, celebrate with your own Olympic games. In the parade, a thirteen-foot-high mechanical statue pours offerings to the gods.

RELIGION. Convince people that you're utterly divine. Have statues of yourself dressed as the goddess Isis put up all over Egypt. Name your son Helios after the Greek sun god and your daughter Selene after the moon goddess.

COINS. Get Antony to put your face on a Roman coin so everyone will know who you are.

BUILDING PROJECTS. Build an enormous new temple called the Caesarium, in honor of Julius Caesar.

At the ceremony, Caesarion is crowned "King of Kings" and now rules Egypt with you, his mother.

Caesarion

Handy Hint

Beware of bad publicity. In Rome, Octavian is spreading lies about you and Antony to encourage the Romans to go to war against you.

Alexander Helios

Cleopatra Selene

Ptolemy Philadelphus

Armenia

Asia Minor

Crete

Cyrenaica

Egypt

Your three children with Antony are each given a kingdom of their own. Alexander Helios is made King of Armenia, Cleopatra Selene is made Queen of Cyrenaica and Crete, and little Ptolemy is made Lord of Asia Minor.

Battle Stations

Octavian tells everyone in Rome that Antony is a traitor. At a festival for Bellona, the Roman goddess of war, he hurls a blood-tipped spear through the air and declares war on both of you.

Soon Octavian's fleet has surrounded you at Actium in Greece. You have 60 galleys of your own but when you see Antony's ships losing, you decide to head for home. Antony sails after you, leaving his other ships behind to carry on. Not surprisingly, they surrender without much of a fight.

RAMMING SPEED. The best way to sink an enemy galley is to ram it, creating a big hole in the side so that the ship sinks quickly. A fast ship makes this easier.

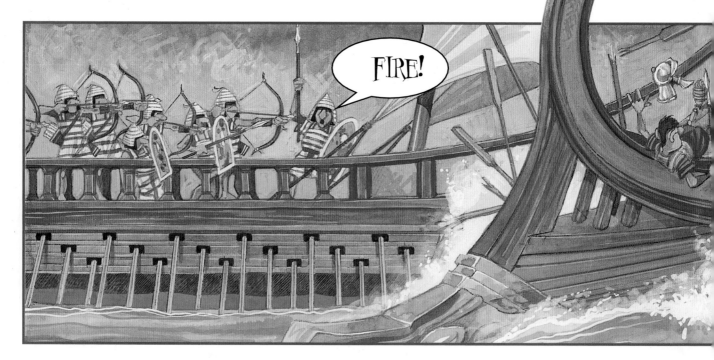

FIRE!

Survive an Ancient Sea Battle—If You Can!

HAND-TO-HAND fighting takes place on deck as soldiers board enemy galleys. Egyptian soldiers use battle axes and hatchets. Romans use short swords and daggers, both useful in a tight corner.

Handy Hint

Ancient sea battles are grim affairs. When the going gets tough—run away!

CRASH!

GIANT CATAPULTS hurl huge rocks or fireballs at enemy ships. When the ships come together, the air is thick with volleys of arrows and sling bullets.

DROWNING is common, since many soldiers cannot swim, especially wearing heavy armor. Sharks attracted by the blood arrive quickly.

Spooked!

Octavian chases you both back to Egypt and soon defeats the rest of your forces at Alexandria. It's all over – Octavian has won. He makes himself the first Roman Emperor, and picks a new name: Augustus.

You shut yourself into a tomb, which is like a small fortress. There is room to hide all your treasure and your servants. Meanwhile, ghostly laughter and footsteps fill the streets and people say that it is Dionysus, Antony's guardian god, dancing out of Alexandria. Antony hears a rumor that you are dead, and in despair he stabs himself with a sword. Hearing this, you ask your slaves to bring Antony to your tomb. He dies in your arms.

The Power of Magic

PEOPLE ARE VERY superstitious in the ancient world. The Egyptians use spells to solve their everyday problems and curses to bring bad luck to their enemies. For them, magic, called "heka," is a good thing. At the beginning of time it helped to create the world and keeps the universe going by guiding the sun god's boat through the underworld.

What Do You Believe?

MUMMIES. Egyptians believe in the afterlife and build tombs for the dead to live in. They preserve dead bodies using chemicals, then wrap them in bandages.

GHOSTS. Romans believe ghosts haunt the houses they lived in when they were alive. To keep bad spirits happy, the head of the house throws black beans over his shoulder.

Do I look dead to you?

No, but I am.

Handy Hint

Unlike Antony, you should always double-check rumors before acting hastily!

CHARMS. Egyptians believe that magic charms can ward off evil spirits. Pregnant women wear a charm depicting Tawaret, the gentle hippo goddess.

SACRED ANIMALS. Egyptians worship animals such as baboons, crocodiles, and cats. A Roman visitor was stoned to death for accidentally killing a cat.

DREAMS have meanings for Egyptians. Dreaming you have the face of a leopard is a good omen! If you dream that your teeth fall out, someone dear to you has died.

Last of the Pharaohs

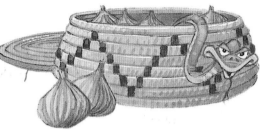

ctavian allows you to give Antony a big funeral. You're afraid, however, that he will take you to back to Rome and parade you through the streets in chains. To avoid this humiliation, you decide to kill yourself. For a final meal, you order a basket of figs. Inside is a deadly snake, an asp, which is also a symbol of the pharaohs. You send a note to Octavian telling him you want to be buried next to Antony. By the time Octavian's guards arrive to stop you, you are already dead, with two tiny bite marks on your arm.

I guess Cleopatra is hiss-tory!

After Your Death

In 30 BC, at the age of 39, you are buried next to Antony. The last of the pharaohs, you have done everything you can to defend Egypt, but it is not enough. Egypt becomes part of the Roman Empire, with Augustus (Octavian) as its ruler.

Handy Hint

Choose your snake carefully—the asp is a symbol of divine royalty and you believe it will give you immortality.

WAXWORKS. A year after your death, Octavian celebrates his conquest of Egypt with a victory parade. You appear in the form of a wax model, complete with asp!

POISON. Some historians say that you tested poisons on slaves to find out which would give you a quick, painless death.

CHILDREN. Caesarion tries to escape to Syria but is betrayed by his tutor and murdered. Your three children with Antony are forced to walk in chains at Octavian's triumph.

EGYPT. After your death, Octavian declares himself pharaoh. On his orders, all statues of you and Antony are destroyed so that the Egyptians will forget you.

LIVING ON. Despite the efforts to remove you from history, you become one of the most famous women who ever lived.

Glossary

Asp This extremely poisonous snake is an Egyptian cobra. The asp was a symbol of kings in ancient Egypt.

Catapult A large siege engine used to hurl huge rocks and burning missiles at enemy forts and ships.

Chief Steward This important ancient Egyptian official was in charge of temples and was often a member of the king's family.

Conspirator Someone who plots secretly with others against somebody else. Sixty conspirators plotted together to kill Julius Caesar.

Courtier A man or woman who works at or spends much of his or her time at a royal court.

Dionysus The Greek god of wine and dancing. Antony dressed as Dionysus to make himself look like a god.

Exile To throw out or ban someone from his own country.

Galley An ancient ship with several rows of oars. The rowers were usually slaves who were chained to benches along the sides.

Henna A reddish brown dye obtained from the leaves of the henna plant.

Hieroglyphics Ancient Egyptian writing that used little pictures as symbols or letters.

Isis The ancient Egyptian goddess of women and children. Cleopatra put up many statues of herself dressed as Isis to remind people she was a goddess.

King Herod Ruler of Palestine thought to be responsible for the Massacre of the Innocents mentioned in the New Testament.

Mummies Dead bodies preserved and wrapped up in linen bandages. The word "mummy" comes from the Arab word for "tar," which was used to preserve bodies.

Ochre A red clay used to make paints or lipsticks.

Papyri The name for documents written on papyrus, a material made from a tall plant like a rush.

Pharaoh The title for ancient Egyptian kings.

Pyramid Some ancient Egyptian kings built giant tombs in the shape of a pyramid – which has a square base and four triangles for sides.

Ra The Egyptian god of the sun, who was shown with the head of a hawk.

Scrolls Documents that can be rolled up.

Superstitious Believing in things that cannot be proved by science, such as fate and magic.

Triumph The name of the victory procession through Rome after an important battle had been won.

Index